Cambridge Plain Texts

JOHNSON

PAPERS FROM
THE IDLER

T0346132

JOHNSON

PAPERS FROM
THE IDLER

CAMBRIDGE
AT THE UNIVERSITY PRESS
1932

CAMBRIDGE UNIVERSITY PRESS
Cambridge, New York, Melbourne, Madrid, Cape Town,
Singapore, São Paulo, Delhi, Mexico City

Cambridge University Press
The Edinburgh Building, Cambridge CB2 8RU, UK

Published in the United States of America by Cambridge University Press, New York

www.cambridge.org
Information on this title: www.cambridge.org/9781107624726

First Edition 1921
Reprinted 1925
       ,,   1931 (twice)
       ,,   1932
First published 1932
Re-issued 2013

A catalogue record for this publication is available from the British Library

ISBN 978-1-107-62472-6 Paperback

NOTE

"*The Idler*" says Boswell "is evidently the work of the same mind which produced *The Rambler*, but has less body and more spirit. It has more variety of real life and greater facility of language."

This comparison would appear to be wholly in *The Idler's* favour, but Boswell (apologetic, as always, when the Sage descends to levity) is careful to explain that "there are in *The Idler* several papers which shew much profundity of thought and labour of language."

Such papers are, for the most part, omitted from the present selection. Instead, we may picture Johnson writing his weekly article ("often as hastily as any ordinary letter") on such familiar topics as the press in war-time, the art of advertisement, the multiplication of books, and the female bargain-hunter; we may read also his character sketches of Jack Whirler (of whom the original was Newbery, the publisher), of Dick Minim, the shallow critic, of Sober, who is Johnson himself.

Of the 103 papers, 12 were contributed by Johnson's friends; one of these (No. 33, by Thomas Warton) is reprinted here as shewing the satirist's view of the eighteenth century don.

The Idler papers served as the principal contributions for two years (1758–60) to *The Universal Chronicle*; only in the last of the series does Johnson's "secret horrour" of human finality obtain the mastery over that lighter spirit which pervades the majority of the essays.

S. C. ROBERTS

December 1920

CONTENTS

THE IDLER

No. 5. SATURDAY, MAY 13, 1758.

————Κάλλος
'Αντ' ἐγχέων ἁπάντων
'Αντ' ἀσπίδων ἁπασῶν.   ANAC.

OUR military operations are at last begun; our troops are marching in all the pomp of war, and a camp is marked out on the Isle of Wight; the heart of every Englishman now swells with confidence, though somewhat softened by generous compassion for the consternation and distresses of our enemies.

This formidable armament and splendid march produce different effects upon different minds, according to the boundless diversities of temper, occupation, and habits of thought.

Many a tender maiden considers her lover as already lost, because he cannot reach the camp but by crossing the sea; men, of a more political understanding, are persuaded that we shall now see, in a few days, the ambassadours of France supplicating for pity. Some are hoping for a bloody battle, because a bloody battle makes a vendible narrative; some are composing songs of victory; some planning arches of triumph; and some are mixing fireworks for the celebration of a peace.

Of all extensive and complicated objects, different parts are selected by different eyes; and minds are variously affected, as they vary their attention. The care of the publick is now fixed upon our soldiers, who are leaving their native country to wander, none can tell how long, in the pathless deserts of the Isle of Wight. The tender sigh for their sufferings, and the gay drink to their success. I, who look, or believe myself to look, with more philosophick eyes on human affairs, must confess, that I saw the troops march with little emotion; my thoughts were fixed upon other scenes, and the tear stole into my eyes, not for those who were going away, but for those who were left behind.

We have no reason to doubt but our troops will proceed with proper caution; there are men among them who can take care of themselves. But how shall the ladies endure without them? By what arts can they, who have long had no joy but from the civilities of a soldier, now amuse their hours, and solace their separation?

Of fifty thousand men, now destined to different stations, if we allow each to have been occasionally necessary only to four women, a short computation will inform us, that two hundred thousand ladies are left to languish in distress; two hundred thousand ladies, who must run to sales and auctions without an attendant; sit at the play, without a critick to direct their opinion; buy their fans by their own judgment; dispose shells by their own invention; walk in the Mall without a gallant; go to the gardens without a protector; and shuffle cards with vain impatience, for want of a fourth to complete the party.

Of these ladies, some, I hope, have lap-dogs, and some monkeys; but they are unsatisfactory companions. Many useful offices are performed by men of scarlet, to which neither dog nor monkey has adequate abilities. A parrot, indeed, is as fine as a colonel, and, if he has been much used to good company, is not wholly without conversation; but a parrot, after all, is a poor little creature, and has neither sword nor shoulder-knot, can neither dance nor play at cards.

Since the soldiers must obey the call of their duty, and go to that side of the kingdom which faces France, I know not why the ladies, who cannot live without them, should not follow them. The prejudices and pride of man have long presumed the sword and spindle made for different hands, and denied the other sex to partake the grandeur of military glory. This notion may be consistently enough received in France, where the salick law excludes females from the throne; but we, who allow them to be sovereigns, may surely suppose them capable to be soldiers.

It were to be wished that some man, whose experience and authority might enforce regard, would propose that our encampments for the present year should comprise an equal number of men and women, who should march and fight in mingled bodies. If proper colonels were once appointed, and the drums ordered to beat for female volunteers, our regiments would soon be filled without the reproach or cruelty of an impress.

Of these heroines, some might serve on foot under the denomination of the *Female Buffs*, and some on horseback, with the title of *Lady Hussars*.

What objections can be made to this scheme I have endeavoured maturely to consider; and cannot find that a modern soldier has any duties, except that of obedience, which a lady cannot perform. If the hair has lost its powder, a lady has a puff; if a coat be spotted, a lady has a brush. Strength is of less importance since fire-arms have been used; blows of the hand are now seldom exchanged; and what is there to be done in the charge or the retreat beyond the powers of a sprightly maiden?

Our masculine squadrons will not suppose themselves disgraced by their auxiliaries, till they have done something which women could not have done. The troops of Braddock never saw their enemies, and perhaps were defeated by women. If our American general had headed an army of girls, he might still have built a fort and taken it. Had Minorca been defended by a female garrison, it might have been surrendered, as it was, without a breach; and I cannot but think, that seven thousand women might have ventured to look at Rochfort, sack a village, rob a vineyard, and return in safety.

No. 7. SATURDAY, MAY 27, 1758.

ONE of the principal amusements of the *Idler* is to read the works of those minute historians the writers of news, who, though contemptuously overlooked by the composers of bulky volumes, are yet necessary in a nation where much wealth produces much leisure, and one part of the people has nothing to do but to observe the lives and fortunes of the other.

To us, who are regaled every morning and evening with intelligence, and are supplied from day to day with materials for conversation, it is difficult to conceive how man can subsist without a newspaper, or to what entertainment companies can assemble, in those wide regions of the earth that have neither *Chronicles* nor *Magazines*, neither *Gazettes* nor *Advertisers*, neither *Journals* nor *Evening Posts*.

There are never great numbers in any nation, whose reason or invention can find employment for their tongues, who can raise a pleasing discourse from their own stock of sentiments and images; and those few who have qualified themselves by speculation for general disquisitions are soon left without an audience. The common talk of men must relate to facts in which the talkers have, or think they have, an interest; and where such facts cannot be known, the pleasures of society will be merely sensual. Thus the natives of the Mahometan empires, who approach most nearly to European civility, have no higher pleasure at their convivial assemblies than to hear a piper, or gaze upon a tumbler; and no company can keep together longer than they are diverted by sounds or shows.

All foreigners remark, that the knowledge of the common people of England is greater than that of any other vulgar. This superiority we undoubtedly owe to the rivulets of intelligence, which are continually trickling among us, which every one may catch, and of which every one partakes.

This universal diffusion of instruction is, perhaps, not wholly without its inconveniencies; it certainly fills the nation with superficial disputants; enables those to talk who were born to work; and affords information sufficient to elate vanity, and stiffen obstinacy, but too little to enlarge the mind into complete skill for full comprehension.

Whatever is found to gratify the publick, will be multiplied by the emulation of venders beyond necessity or use. This plenty indeed produces cheapness, but cheapness always ends in negligence and depravation.

The compilation of newspapers is often committed to narrow and mercenary minds, not qualified for the task of delighting or instructing; who are content to fill their paper, with whatever matter, without industry to gather, or discernment to select.

Thus journals are daily multiplied without increase of knowledge. The tale of the morning paper is told again in the evening, and the narratives of the evening are bought again in the morning. These repetitions, indeed, waste time, but they do not shorten it. The most eager peruser of news is tired before he has completed his labour; and many a man, who enters the coffee-house in his night-gown and slippers, is called away to his shop, or his dinner, before he has well considered the state of Europe.

It is discovered by Reaumur, that spiders might make silk, if they could be persuaded to live in peace together. The writers of news, if they could be confederated, might give more pleasure to the publick. The morning and evening authors might divide an event between them; a single action, and that not of much importance, might be gradually discovered, so as to vary a whole week with joy, anxiety, and conjecture.

We know that a French ship of war was lately taken by a ship of England; but this event was suffered to burst upon us all at once, and then what we knew already was echoed from day to day, and from week to week.

Let us suppose these spiders of literature to spin

together, and inquire to what an extensive web such
another event might be regularly drawn, and how six
morning and six evening writers might agree to retail
their articles.

On *Monday Morning* the Captain of a ship might
arrive, who left the *Friseur* of *France*, and the *Bull-
dog*, Captain *Grim*, in sight of one another, so that an
engagement seemed unavoidable.

Monday Evening. A sound of cannon was heard off
Cape Finisterre, supposed to be those of the Bull-dog
and Friseur.

Tuesday Morning. It was this morning reported
that the Bull-dog engaged the Friseur, yard-arm and
yard-arm, three glasses and a half, but was obliged to
sheer off for want of powder. It is hoped that inquiry
will be made into this affair in a proper place.

Tuesday Evening. The account of the engagement
between the Bull-dog and Friseur was premature.

Wednesday Morning. Another express is arrived,
which brings news, that the Friseur had lost all her
masts, and three hundred of her men, in the late
engagement; and that Captain Grim is come into
harbour much shattered.

Wednesday Evening. We hear that the brave Captain Grim, having expended his powder, proposed to
enter the Friseur sword in hand; but that his lieu-
tenant, the nephew of a certain nobleman, remon-
strated against it.

Thursday Morning. We wait impatiently for a full
account of the late engagement between the Bull-dog
and Friseur.

Thursday Evening. It is said the order of the Bath
will be sent to Captain Grim.

Friday Morning. A certain Lord of the Admiralty has been heard to say of a certain Captain, that if he had done his duty, a certain French ship might have been taken. It was not thus that merit was rewarded in the days of Cromwell.

Friday Evening. There is certain information at the Admiralty, that the Friseur is taken, after a resistance of two hours.

Saturday Morning. A letter from one of the gunners of the Bull-dog mentions the taking of the Friseur, and attributes their success wholly to the bravery and resolution of Captain Grim, who never owed any of his advancement to borough-jobbers, or any other corrupters of the people.

Saturday Evening. Captain Grim arrived at the Admiralty, with an account that he engaged the Friseur, a ship of equal force with his own, off Cape Finisterre, and took her after an obstinate resistance, having killed one hundred and fifty of the French, with the loss of ninety-five of his own men.

No. 19. SATURDAY, AUGUST 19, 1758.

SOME of those ancient sages that have exercised their abilities in the inquiry after the *supreme good*, have been of opinion, that the highest degree of earthly happiness is quiet; a calm repose both of mind and body, undisturbed by the sight of folly or the noise of business, the tumults of publick commotion, or the agitations of private interest: a state in which the mind has no other employment, but to observe and regulate her own motions, to trace thought from thought, combine one image with another, raise systems of science, and form theories of virtue.

To the scheme of these solitary speculatists, it has been justly objected, that if they are happy, they are happy only by being useless. That mankind is one vast republick, where every individual receives many benefits from the labours of others, which, by labouring in his turn for others, he is obliged to repay; and that where the united efforts of all are not able to exempt all from misery, none have a right to withdraw from their task of vigilance, or to be indulged in idle wisdom or solitary pleasures.

It is common for controvertists, in the heat of disputation, to add one position to another till they reach the extremities of knowledge, where truth and falsehood lose their distinction. Their admirers follow them to the brink of absurdity, and then start back from each side towards the middle point. So it has happened in this great disquisition. Many perceive alike the force of the contrary arguments, find quiet shameful, and business dangerous, and therefore pass their lives between them, in bustle without business, and negligence without quiet.

Among the principal names of this moderate set is that great philosopher Jack Whirler, whose business keeps him in perpetual motion, and whose motion always eludes his business; who is always to do what he never does, who cannot stand still because he is wanted in another place, and who is wanted in many places because he stays in none.

Jack has more business than he can conveniently transact in one house; he has therefore one habitation near Bow-church, and another about a mile distant.

By this ingenious distribution of himself between two houses, Jack has contrived to be found at neither. Jack's trade is extensive, and he has many dealers; his conversation is sprightly, and he has many companions; his disposition is kind, and he has many friends. Jack neither forbears pleasure for business, nor omits business for pleasure, but is equally invisible to his friends and his customers; to him that comes with an invitation to a club, and to him that waits to settle an account.

When you call at his house, his clerk tells you that Mr. Whirler has just stept out, but will be at home exactly at two; you wait at a coffee-house till two, and then find that he has been at home, and is gone out again, but left word that he should be at the Half-moon tavern at seven, where he hopes to meet you. At seven you go to the tavern. At eight in comes Mr. Whirler to tell you that he is glad to see you, and only begs leave to run for a few minutes to a gentleman that lives near the Exchange, from whom he will return before supper can be ready. Away he runs to the Exchange, to tell those who are waiting for him that he must beg them to defer the business till to-morrow, because his time is come at the Half-moon.

Jack's cheerfulness and civility rank him among those whose presence never gives pain, and whom all receive with fondness and caresses. He calls often on his friends, to tell them that he will come again to-morrow; on the morrow he comes again, to tell them how an unexpected summons hurries him away. —When he enters a house, his first declaration is, that he cannot sit down; and so short are his visits, that he seldom appears to have come for any other reason, but to say, He must go.

The dogs of Egypt, when thirst brings them to the Nile, are said to run as they drink for fear of the crocodiles. Jack Whirler always dines at full speed. He enters, finds the family at table, sits familiarly down, and fills his plate; but while the first morsel is in his mouth, hears the clock strike, and rises; then goes to another house, sits down again, recollects another engagement, has only time to taste the soup, makes a short excuse to the company, and continues through another street his desultory dinner.

But, overwhelmed as he is with business, his chief desire is to have still more. Every new proposal takes possession of his thoughts; he soon balances probabilities, engages in the project, brings it almost to completion, and then forsakes it for another, which he catches with the same alacrity, urges with the same vehemence, and abandons with the same coldness.

Every man may be observed to have a certain strain of lamentation, some peculiar theme of complaint, on which he dwells in his moments of dejection. Jack's topick of sorrow is the want of time. Many an excellent design languishes in empty theory for want of time. For the omission of any civilities, want of time is his plea to others; for the neglect of any affairs, want of time is his excuse to himself. That he wants time, he sincerely believes; for he once pined away many months with a lingering distemper, for want of time to attend to his health.

Thus Jack Whirler lives in perpetual fatigue without proportionate advantage, because he does not consider that no man can see all with his own eyes, or do all with his own hands; that whoever is engaged in multiplicity of business, must transact much by substitution, and leave something to hazard; and that he who attempts to do all, will waste his life in doing little.

No. 30. SATURDAY, NOVEMBER 11, 1758.

THE desires of man increase with his acquisitions; every step which he advances brings something within his view, which he did not see before, and which, as soon as he sees it, he begins to want. Where necessity ends, curiosity begins; and no sooner are we supplied with every thing that nature can demand, than we sit down to contrive artificial appetites.

By this restlessness of mind, every populous and wealthy city is filled with innumerable employments, for which the greater part of mankind is without a name; with artificers, whose labour is exerted in producing such petty conveniencies, that many shops are furnished with instruments, of which the use can hardly be found without inquiry, but which he that once knows them quickly learns to number among necessary things.

Such is the diligence with which, in countries completely civilized, one part of mankind labours for another, that wants are supplied faster than they can be formed, and the idle and luxurious find life stagnate for want of some desire to keep it in motion. This species of distress furnishes a new set of occupations; and multitudes are busied, from day to day, in finding the rich and the fortunate something to do.

It is very common to reproach those artists as useless, who produce only such superfluities as neither accommodate the body, nor improve the mind; and of which no other effect can be imagined, than that they are the occasions of spending money, and consuming time.

But this censure will be mitigated, when it is seriously considered, that money and time are the heaviest burdens of life, and that the unhappiest of all mortals are those who have more of either than they know how to use. To set himself free from these incumbrances, one hurries to Newmarket; another travels over Europe; one pulls down his house and calls architects about him; another buys a seat in the country, and follows his hounds over hedges and through rivers; one makes collections of shells; and another searches the world for tulips and carnations.

He is surely a publick benefactor who finds employment for those to whom it is thus difficult to find it for themselves. It is true, that this is seldom done merely from generosity or compassion; almost every man seeks his own advantage in helping others, and therefore it is too common for mercenary officiousness to consider rather what is grateful, than what is right.

We all know that it is more profitable to be loved than esteemed; and ministers of pleasure will always be found, who study to make themselves necessary, and to supplant those who are practising the same arts.

One of the amusements of idleness is reading without the fatigue of close attention, and the world therefore swarms with writers whose wish is not to be studied, but to be read.

No species of literary men has lately been so much multiplied as the writers of news. Not many years ago the nation was content with one gazette; but now we have not only in the metropolis papers for every morning and every evening, but almost every large town has its weekly historian, who regularly circulates his periodical intelligence, and fills the villages of his district with conjectures on the events of war, and with debates on the true interest of Europe.

To write news in its perfection requires such a combination of qualities, that a man completely fitted for the task is not always to be found. In Sir Henry Wotton's jocular definition, *An ambassador* is said to be *a man of virtue sent abroad to tell lies for the advantage of his country;* a news-writer is *a man without virtue, who writes lies at home for his own profit*. To these compositions is required neither genius nor knowledge, neither industry nor sprightliness; but contempt of shame and indifference to truth are absolutely necessary. He who by a long familiarity with infamy has obtained these qualities, may confidently tell to-day what he intends to contradict to-morrow; he may affirm fearlessly what he knows that he shall be obliged to recant, and may write letters from Amsterdam or Dresden to himself.

In a time of war the nation is always of one mind, eager to hear something good of themselves and ill of the enemy. At this time the task of news-writers is easy: they have nothing to do but to tell that a battle is expected, and afterwards that a battle has been fought, in which we and our friends, whether conquering or conquered, did all, and our enemies did nothing.

Scarcely any thing awakens attention like a tale of cruelty. The writer of news never fails in the intermission of action to tell how the enemies murdered

children and ravished virgins; and, if the scene of
action be somewhat distant, scalps half the inhabitants
of a province.

Among the calamities of war may be justly num-
bered the diminution of the love of truth, by the
falsehoods which interest dictates, and credulity en-
courages. A peace will equally leave the warriour and
relater of wars destitute of employment; and I know
not whether more is to be dreaded from streets filled
with soldiers accustomed to plunder, or from garrets
filled with scribblers accustomed to lie.

No. 31. SATURDAY, NOVEMBER 18, 1758.

MANY moralists have remarked, that pride has of all
human vices the widest dominion, appears in the
greatest multiplicity of forms, and lies hid under the
greatest variety of disguises; of disguises, which, like
the moon's *veil of brightness*, are both its *lustre and its
shade*, and betray it to others, though they hide it
from ourselves.

It is not my intention to degrade pride from this
pre-eminence of mischief; yet I know not whether
idleness may not maintain a very doubtful and obstinate competition.

There are some that profess idleness in its full
dignity, who call themselves the *Idle*, as Busiris in
the play calls himself the *Proud*; who boast that they
do nothing, and thank their stars that they have
nothing to do; who sleep every night till they can
sleep not longer, and rise only that exercise may
enable them to sleep again; who prolong the reign of
darkness by double curtains, and never see the sun

but to *tell him how they hate his beams*; whose whole labour is to vary the posture of indolence, and whose day differs from their night, but as a couch or chair differs from a bed.

These are the true and open votaries of idleness, for whom she weaves the garlands of poppies, and into whose cup she pours the waters of oblivion; who exist in a state of unruffled stupidity, forgetting and forgotten; who have long ceased to live, and at whose death the survivors can only say, that they have ceased to breathe.

But idleness predominates in many lives where it is not suspected; for, being a vice which terminates in itself, it may be enjoyed without injury to others; and it is therefore not watched like fraud, which endangers property; or like pride, which naturally seeks its gratifications in another's inferiority. Idleness is a silent and peaceful quality, that neither raises envy by ostentation, nor hatred by opposition; and therefore nobody is busy to censure or detect it.

As pride sometimes is hid under humility, idleness is often covered by turbulence and hurry. He that neglects his known duty and real employment, naturally endeavours to crowd his mind with something that may bar out the remembrance of his own folly, and does any thing but what he ought to do with eager diligence, that he may keep himself in his own favour.

Some are always in a state of preparation, occupied in previous measures, forming plans, accumulating materials, and providing for the main affair. These are certainly under the secret power of idleness. Nothing is to be expected from the workman whose tools are for ever to be sought. I was once told by a great master, that no man ever excelled in paint-ing, who was eminently curious about pencils and colours.

There are others to whom idleness dictates another expedient, by which life may be passed unprofitably away without the tediousness of many vacant hours. The art is, to fill the day with petty business, to have always something in hand which may raise curiosity, but not solicitude, and keep the mind in a state of action, but not of labour.

This art has for many years been practised by my old friend Sober with wonderful success. Sober is a man of strong desires and quick imagination, so exactly balanced by the love of ease, that they can seldom stimulate him to any difficult undertaking; they have, however, so much power, that they will not suffer him to lie quite at rest; and though they do not make him sufficiently useful to others, they make him at least weary of himself.

Mr. Sober's chief pleasure is conversation; there is no end of his talk or his attention; to speak or to hear is equally pleasing; for he still fancies that he is teach-ing or learning something, and is free for the time from his own reproaches.

But there is one time at night when he must go home, that his friends may sleep; and another time in the morning, when all the world agrees to shut out interruption. These are the moments of which poor Sober trembles at the thought. But the misery of these tiresome intervals he has many means of allevi-ating. He has persuaded himself that the manual arts are undeservedly overlooked; he has observed in many trades the effects of close thought, and just ratiocination. From speculation he proceeded to practice, and supplied himself with the tools of a carpenter, with which he mended his coal-box very successfully, and which he still continues to employ, as he finds occasion.

He has attempted at other times the crafts of the shoemaker, tinman, plumber, and potter; in all these arts he has failed, and resolves to qualify himself for them by better information. But his daily amusement is chymistry. He has a small furnace, which he employs in distillation, and which has long been the solace of his life. He draws oils and waters, and essences and spirits, which he knows to be of no use; sits and counts the drops, as they come from his retort, and forgets that, whilst a drop is falling, a moment flies away.

Poor Sober! I have often teased him with reproof, and he has often promised reformation; for no man is so much open to conviction as the Idler, but there is none on whom it operates so little. What will be the effect of this paper I know not; perhaps, he will read it and laugh, and light the fire in his furnace; but my hope is, that he will quit his trifles, and betake himself to rational and useful diligence.

No. 33. SATURDAY, DECEMBER 2, 1758.

[I hope the author of the following letter[1] will excuse
the omission of some parts, and allow me to remark,
that the Journal of the Citizen in the *Spectator* has
almost precluded the attempt of any future writer.]

> ———*Non ita Romuli*
> *Præscriptum, et intonsi Catonis*
> *Auspiciis, veterumque normâ.*
> Hor. Lib. ii. Ode xv. 10.

Sir,

        You have often solicited correspondence. I
have sent you the Journal of a Senior Fellow, or
Genuine Idler, just transmitted from Cambridge by
a facetious correspondent, and warranted to have
been transcribed from the common-place book of the
journalist.

Monday, Nine o'Clock. Turned off my bed-maker
for waking me at eight. Weather rainy. Consulted
my weather-glass. No hopes of a ride before dinner.

Ditto, Ten. After breakfast, transcribed half a
sermon from Dr. Hickman. N.B. Never to transcribe
any more from Calamy; Mrs. Pilcocks, at my curacy,
having one volume of that author lying in her parlour-
window.

Ditto, Eleven. Went down into my cellar. Mem.
My Mountain will be fit to drink in a month's time.
N.B. To remove the five-year old port into the new
bin on the left hand.

Ditto, Twelve. Mended a pen. Looked at my
weather-glass again. Quicksilver very low. Shaved.
Barber's hand shakes.

[1] Thomas Warton.

Ditto, One. Dined alone in my room on a sole. N.B. The shrimp-sauce not so good as Mr. H. of Peterhouse and I used to eat in London last winter at the Mitre in Fleet-street. Sat down to a pint of Madeira. Mr. H. surprised me over it. We finished two bottles of port together, and were very cheerful. Mem. To dine with Mr. H. at Perterhouse next Wednesday. One of the dishes a leg of pork and pease, by my desire.

Ditto, Six. Newspaper in the common room.

Ditto, Seven. Returned to my room. Made a tiff of warm punch, and to bed before nine; did not fall asleep till ten, a young fellow commoner being very noisy over my head.

Tuesday, Nine. Rose squeamish. A fine morning. Weather-glass very high.

Ditto, Ten. Ordered my horse, and rode to the five-mile stone on the Newmarket road. Appetite gets better. A pack of hounds, in full cry, crossed the road, and startled my horse.

Ditto, Twelve. Drest. Found a letter on my table to be in London the 19th inst. Bespoke a new wig.

Ditto, One. At dinner in the hall. Too much water in the soup. Dr. Dry always orders the beef to be salted too much for me.

Ditto, Two. In the common room. Dr. Dry gave us an instance of a gentleman who kept the gout out of his stomach by drinking old Madeira. Conversation chiefly on the expeditions. Company broke up at four. Dr. Dry and myself played at backgammon for a brace of snipes. Won.

Ditto, Five. At the coffee-house. Met Mr. H. there. Could not get a sight of the Monitor.

Ditto, Seven. Returned home, and stirred my fire. Went to the common room, and supped on the snipes with Dr. Dry.

Ditto, Eight. Began the evening in the common room. Dr. Dry told several stories. Were very merry. Our new fellow, that studies physick, very talkative toward twelve. Pretends he will bring the youngest Miss —— to drink tea with me soon. Impertinent blockhead!

Wednesday, Nine. Alarmed with a pain in my ankle. Q. The gout? Fear I can't dine at Peterhouse; but I hope a ride will set all to rights. Weather-glass below Fair.

Ditto, Ten. Mounted my horse, though the weather suspicious. Pain in my ankle entirely gone. Caught in a shower coming back. Convinced that my weather-glass is the best in Cambridge.

Ditto, Twelve. Drest. Sauntered up to the Fish-monger's hill. Met Mr. H. and went with him to Peterhouse. Cook made us wait thirty-six minutes beyond the time. The company, some of my Emmanuel friends. For dinner, a pair of soles, a leg of pork and pease, among other things. Mem. Pease-pudding not boiled enough. Cook reprimanded and sconced in my presence.

Ditto, after Dinner. Pain in my ankle returns. Dull all the afternoon. Rallied for being no company. Mr. H.'s account of the accommodations on the road in his Bath journey.

Ditto, Six. Got into spirits. Never was more chatty. We sat late at whist. Mr. H. and self agreed at parting to take a gentle ride, and dine at the old house on the London road to-morrow.

Thursday, Nine. My sempstress. She has lost the measure of my wrist. Forced to be measured again. The baggage has got a trick of smiling.

Ditto, Ten to Eleven. Made some rappee snuff. Read the magazines. Received a present of pickles from Miss Pilcocks. Mem. To send in return some collared eel, which I know both the old lady and miss are fond of.

Ditto, Eleven. Glass very high. Mounted at the gate with Mr. H. Horse skittish, and wants exercise. Arrive at the old house. All the provisions bespoke by some rakish fellow-commoner in the next room, who had been on a scheme to Newmarket. Could get nothing but mutton-chops off the worst end. Port very new. Agree to try some other house to-morrow.

Here the journal breaks off: for the next morning, as my friend informs me, our genial academick was waked with a severe fit of the gout; and, at present, enjoys all the dignity of that disease. But I believe we have lost nothing by this interruption: since a continuation of the remainder of the journal, through the remainder of the week, would most probably have exhibited nothing more than a repeated relation of the same circumstances of idling and luxury.

I hope it will not be concluded, from this specimen of academick life, that I have attempted to decry our universities. If literature is not the essential requisite of the modern academick, I am yet persuaded, that Cambridge and Oxford, however degenerated, surpass the fashionable *academies* of our metropolis, and the *gymnasia* of foreign countries. The number of learned persons in these celebrated seats is still considerable, and more conveniencies and opportunities for study still subsist in them, than in any other place. There is at least one very powerful incentive to learning; I mean the GENIUS *of the place*. It is a sort of inspiring deity, which every youth of quick sensibility and ingenious disposition creates to himself, by reflecting, that he is placed under those venerable walls, where a HOOKER and a HAMMOND, a BACON and a NEWTON, once pursued the same course of science, and from whence they soared to the most elevated heights of literary fame. This is that incitement which Tully, according to his own testimony, experienced at Athens, when he contemplated the porticos where Socrates sat, and the laurel-groves where Plato disputed. But there are other circumstances, and of the highest importance, which render our colleges superior to all other places of education. Their institutions, although somewhat fallen from their primæval simplicity, are such as influence, in a particular manner, the moral conduct of their youth; and in this general depravity of manners and laxity of principles, pure religion is no where more strongly inculcated. The *academies*, as they are presumptuously styled, are too low to be mentioned; and foreign seminaries are likely to prejudice the unwary mind with Calvinism. But English universities render their students virtuous, at least by excluding all opportunities of vice; and, by teaching them the principles of the Church of England, confirm them in those of true Christianity.

No. 34. SATURDAY, DECEMBER 9, 1758.

To illustrate one thing by its resemblance to another, has been always the most popular and efficacious art of instruction. There is indeed no other method of teaching that of which any one is ignorant, but by means of something already known; and a mind so enlarged by contemplation, and inquiry, that it has always many objects within its view, will seldom be long without some near and familiar image through which an easy transition may be made to truths more distant and obscure.

Of the parallels which have been drawn by wit and curiosity, some are literal and real, as between poetry and painting, two arts which pursue the same end, by the operation of the same mental faculties, and which differ only as the one represents things by marks permanent and natural, the other by signs accidental and arbitrary. The one, therefore, is more easily and generally understood, since similitude of form is immediately perceived; the other is capable of conveying more ideas, for men have thought and spoken of many things which they do not see.

Other parallels are fortuitous and fanciful, yet these have sometimes been extended to many particulars of resemblance by a lucky concurrence of diligence and chance. The animal body is composed of many members, united under the direction of one mind: any number of individuals, connected for some common purpose, is therefore called a body. From this participation of the same appellation arose the comparison of the body natural and body politick, of which, how far soever it has been deduced, no end has hitherto been found.

In these imaginary similitudes, the same word is used at once in its primitive and metaphorical sense. Thus health, ascribed to the body natural, is opposed to sickness; but attributed to the body politick stands as contrary to adversity. These parallels therefore have more of genius, but less of truth; they often please, but they never convince.

Of this kind is a curious speculation frequently indulged by a philosopher of my acquaintance, who had discovered, that the qualities requisite to conversation are very exactly represented by a bowl of punch.

Punch, says this profound investigator, is a liquor compounded of spirit and acid juices, sugar and water. The spirit, volatile and fiery, is the proper emblem of vivacity and wit; the acidity of the lemon will very aptly figure pungency of raillery, and acrimony of censure; sugar is the natural representative of luscious adulation and gentle complaisance; and water is the proper hieroglyphick of easy prattle, innocent and tasteless.

Spirit alone is too powerful for use. It will produce madness rather than merriment; and instead of quenching thirst will inflame the blood. Thus wit, too copiously poured out, agitates the hearer with emotions rather violent than pleasing; every one shrinks from the force of its oppression, the company sits entranced and overpowered; all are astonished, but nobody is pleased.

The acid juices give this genial liquor all its power of stimulating the palate. Conversation would become dull and vapid, if negligence were not sometimes roused, and sluggishness quickened, by due severity of reprehension. But acids unmixed will distort the face and torture the palate; and he that has no other qualities than penetration and asperity, he whose constant employment is detection and censure, who looks only to find faults, and speaks only to punish them, will soon be dreaded, hated and avoided.

The taste of sugar is generally pleasing, but it cannot long be eaten by itself. Thus meekness and courtesy will always recommend the first address, but soon pall and nauseate, unless they are associated with more sprightly qualities. The chief use of sugar is to temper the taste of other substances; and softness of behaviour, in the same manner, mitigates the roughness of contradiction, and allays the bitterness of unwelcome truth.

Water is the universal vehicle by which are conveyed the particles necessary to sustenance and growth, by which thirst is quenched, and all the wants of life and nature are supplied. Thus all the business of the world is transacted by artless and easy talk, neither sublimed by fancy, nor discoloured by affectation, without either the harshness of satire, or the lusciousness of flattery. By this limpid vein of language, curiosity is gratified, and all the knowledge is conveyed which one man is required to impart for the safety or convenience of another. Water is the only ingredient in punch which can be used alone, and with which man is content till fancy has framed an artificial want. Thus while we only desire to have our ignorance informed, we are most delighted with the plainest diction; and it is only in the moments of idleness or pride, that we call for the gratifications of wit or flattery.

He only will please long, who, by tempering the acidity of satire with the sugar of civility, and allaying the heat of wit with the frigidity of humble chat, can make the true punch of conversation; and, as that punch can be drunk in the greatest quantity which has the largest proportion of water, so that companion will be oftenest welcome, whose talk flows out with inoffensive copiousness, and unenvied insipidity.

No. 35. SATURDAY, DECEMBER 16, 1758.

TO THE IDLER.

Mr. Idler,

If it be difficult to persuade the idle to be busy, it is likewise, as experience has taught me, not easy to convince the busy that it is better to be idle. When you shall despair of stimulating sluggishness to motion, I hope you will turn your thoughts towards the means of stilling the bustle of pernicious activity.

I am the unfortunate husband of a *buyer of bargains*. My wife has somewhere heard, that a good housewife *never* has any thing to *purchase when it is wanted*. This maxim is often in her mouth, and always in her head. She is not one of those philosophical talkers that speculate without practice; and learn sentences of wisdom only to repeat them: she is always making additions to her stores; she never looks into a broker's shop, but she spies something that may be wanted some time; and it is impossible to make her pass the door of a house where she hears *goods selling by auction*.

Whatever she thinks cheap, she holds it the duty of an economist to buy; in consequence of this maxim, we are encumbered on every side with useless lumber. The servants can scarcely creep to their beds through the chests and boxes that surround them. The carpenter is employed once a week in building closets, fixing cupboards, and fastening shelves; and my house has the appearance of a ship stored for a voyage to the colonies.

I had often observed that advertisements set her on fire; and therefore, pretending to emulate her laudable frugality, I forbade the newspaper to be taken any longer; but my precaution is vain; I know not by what fatality, or by what confederacy, every catalogue of *genuine furniture* comes to her hand, every advertisement of a warehouse newly opened, is in her pocket-book, and she knows before any of her neighbours when the stock of any man *leaving off trade* is to be *sold cheap for ready money*.

Such intelligence is to my dear-one the Syren's song. No engagement, no duty, no interest, can withhold her from a sale, from which she always returns congratulating herself upon her dexterity at a bargain; the porter lays down his burden in the hall; she displays her new acquisitions, and spends the rest of the day in contriving where they shall be put.

As she cannot bear to have any thing uncomplete, one purchase necessitates another; she has twenty feather-beds more than she can use, and a late sale has supplied her with a proportionable number of Witney blankets, a large roll of linen for sheets, and five quilts for every bed, which she bought because the seller told her, that if she would clear his hands he would let her have a bargain.

Thus by hourly encroachments my habitation is made narrower and narrower; the dining-room is so crowded with tables, that dinner scarcely can be served; the parlour is decorated with so many piles of china, that I dare not step within the door; at every turn of the stairs I have a clock, and half the windows of the upper floors are darkened, that shelves may be set before them.

This, however, might be borne, if she would gratify her own inclinations without opposing mine. But I, who am idle, am luxurious, and she condemns me to live upon salt provisions. She knows the loss of buying in small quantities, we have, therefore, whole hogs and quarters of oxen. Part of our meat is tainted before it is eaten, and part is thrown away because it is spoiled; but she persists in her system, and will never buy any thing by single pennyworths.

The common vice of those who are still grasping at more, is to neglect that which they already possess; but from this failing my charmer is free. It is the great care of her life that the pieces of beef should be boiled in the order in which they are bought; that the second bag of pease should not be opened till the first be eaten; that every feather-bed should be lain on in its turn; that the carpets should be taken out of the chests once a month and brushed, and the rolls of linen opened now and then before the fire. She is daily inquiring after the best traps for mice, and keeps the rooms always scented by fumigations to destroy the moths. She employs workmen, from time to time, to adjust six clocks that never go, and clean five jacks that rust in the garret; and a woman in the next alley lives by scouring the brass and pewter, which are only laid up to tarnish again.

She is always imagining some distant time, in which she shall use whatever she accumulates: she has four looking-glasses which she cannot hang up in her house, but which will be handsome in more lofty rooms; and pays rent for the place of a vast copper in some ware-house, because, when we live in the country, we shall brew our own beer.

Of this life I have long been weary, but know not how to change it: all the married men whom I consult advise me to have patience; but some old bachelors are of opinion that, since she loves sales so well, she should have a sale of her own; and I have, I think, resolved to open her hoards, and advertise an auction.

I am, Sir,

Your very humble servant,

PETER PLENTY.

No. 40. SATURDAY, JANUARY 20, 1759.

THE practice of appending to the narratives of publick transactions more minute and domestick intelligence, and filling the newspapers with advertisements, has grown up by slow degrees to its present state.

Genius is shown only by invention. The man who first took advantage of the general curiosity that was excited by a siege or battle, to betray the readers of news into the knowledge of the shop where the best puffs and powder were to be sold, was undoubtedly a man of great sagacity, and profound skill in the nature of man. But when he had once shown the way, it was easy to follow him; and every man now knows a ready method of informing the publick of all that he desires to buy or sell; whether his wares be material or intellectual; whether he makes clothes, or teaches the mathematicks; whether he be a tutor that wants a pupil, or a pupil that wants a tutor.

Whatever is common is despised. Advertisements

are now so numerous that they are very negligently perused, and it is, therefore, become necessary to gain attention by magnificence of promises, and by eloquence sometimes sublime and sometimes pathetick.

Promise, large promise, is the soul of an advertisement. I remember a *wash-ball* that had a quality truly wonderful—it gave *an exquisite edge to the razor*. And there are now to be sold, *for ready money only*, some *duvets for bed-coverings, of down, beyond comparison superior to what is called otter-down*, and indeed such, that its *many excellencies cannot be here set forth*. With one excellence we are made acquainted—*it is warmer than four or five blankets, and lighter than one.*

There are some, however, that know the prejudice of mankind in favour of modest sincerity. The vender of the *beautifying fluid* sells a lotion that repels pimples, washes away freckles, smooths the skin, and plumps the flesh; and yet, with a generous abhorrence of ostentation, confesses, that it will not *restore the bloom of fifteen to a lady of fifty.*

The true pathos of advertisements must have sunk deep into the heart of every man that remembers the zeal shown by the seller of the *anodyne necklace*, for the ease and safety *of poor teething infants*, and the affection with which he warned every mother, that *she would never forgive herself*, if her infant should perish without a necklace.

I cannot but remark to the celebrated author who gave, in his notifications of the camel and dromedary, so many specimens of the genuine sublime, that there is now arrived another subject yet more worthy of his pen. *A famous Mohawk Indian warrior, who took* Dieskaw *the French general prisoner, dressed in the same manner with the native Indians when they go to war, with his face and body painted, with his scalping-knife, tom-axe, and all other implements of war! a sight worthy the curiosity of every true Briton!* This is a very powerful description; but a critick of great refinement would say, that it conveys rather *horrour* than *terrour*. An Indian, dressed as he goes to war, may bring company together; but if he carries the scalping-knife and tom-axe, there are many true Britons that will never be persuaded to see him but through a grate.

It has been remarked by the severer judges, that the salutary sorrow of tragick scenes is too soon effaced by the merriment of the epilogue; the same inconvenience arises from the improper disposition of advertisements. The noblest objects may be so associated as to be made ridiculous. The camel and dromedary themselves might have lost much of their dignity between *the true flower of mustard* and the *original Daffy's elixir*; and I could not but feel some indignation when I found this illustrious Indian warrior immediately succeeded by *a fresh parcel of Dublin butter*.

The trade of advertising is now so near to perfection, that it is not easy to propose any improvement. But as every art ought to be exercised in due subordination to the publick good, I cannot but propose it as a moral question to these masters of the publick ear, Whether they do not sometimes play too wantonly with our passions, as when the registrar of lottery-tickets invites us to his shop by an account of the prize which he sold last year; and whether the advertising controvertists do not indulge asperity of language without any adequate provocation; as in the dispute about *straps for razors*, now happily subsided, and in the altercation which at present subsists concerning *eau de luce*?

In an advertisement it is allowed to every man to speak well of himself, but I know not why he should assume the privilege of censuring his neighbour. He may proclaim his own virtue or skill, but ought not to exclude others from the same pretensions.

Every man that advertises his own excellence should write with some consciousness of a character which dares to call the attention of the publick. He should remember that his name is to stand in the same paper with those of the king of Prussia and the emperour of Germany, and endeavour to make himself worthy of such association.

Some regard is likewise to be paid to posterity. There are men of diligence and curiosity who treasure up the papers of the day merely because others neglect them, and in time they will be scarce. When these collections shall be read in another century, how will numberless contradictions be reconciled? and how shall fame be possibly distributed among the tailors and bodice-makers of the present age?

Surely these things deserve consideration. It is enough for me to have hinted my desire that these abuses may be rectified; but such is the state of nature, that what all have the right of doing, many will attempt without sufficient care or due qualifications.

No. 55. SATURDAY, MAY 5, 1759.

TO THE IDLER.

MR. IDLER,

I HAVE taken the liberty of laying before you my complaint, and of desiring advice or consolation with the greater confidence, because I believe many other writers have suffered the same indignities with myself, and hope my quarrel will be regarded by you and your readers as the common cause of literature.

Having been long a student, I thought myself qualified in time to become an author. My inquiries have been much diversified and far extended, and not finding my genius directing me by irresistible impulse to any particular subject, I deliberated three years which part of knowledge to illustrate by my labours. Choice is more often determined by accident than by reason: I walked abroad one morning with a curious lady, and, by her inquiries and observations, was incited to write the natural history of the country in which I reside.

Natural history is no work for one that loves his chair or his bed. Speculation may be pursued on a soft couch, but nature must be observed in the open air. I have collected materials with indefatigable pertinacity. I have gathered glow-worms in the evening, and snails in the morning; I have seen the daisy close and open, I have heard the owl shriek at midnight, and hunted insects in the heat of noon.

Seven years I was employed in collecting animals and vegetables, and then found that my design was yet imperfect. The subterranean treasures of the place had been passed unobserved, and another year was to be spent in mines and coal-pits. What I had already

done supplied a sufficient motive to do more. I
acquainted myself with the black inhabitants of metal-
lick caverns, and, in defiance of damps and floods,
wandered through the gloomy labyrinths, and gathered
fossils from every fissure.

At last I began to write, and as I finished any
section of my book, read it to such of my friends, as
were most skilful in the matter which it treated. None
of them were satisfied; one disliked the disposition of
the parts, another the colours of the style; one advised
me to enlarge, another to abridge. I resolved to read
no more, but to take my own way and write on, for
by consultation I only perplexed my thoughts and
retarded my work.

The book was at last finished, and I did not doubt
but my labour would be repaid by profit, and my
ambition satisfied with honours. I considered that
natural history is neither temporary nor local, and
that though I limited my inquiries to my own country,
yet every part of the earth has productions common to
all the rest. Civil history may be partially studied, the
revolutions of one nation may be neglected by another;
but after that in which all have an interest, all must be
inquisitive. No man can have sunk so far into stupidity
as not to consider the properties of the ground on
which he walks, of the plants on which he feeds, or
the animals that delight his ear, or amuse his eye;
and, therefore, I computed that universal curiosity
would call for many editions of my book, and that in
five years I should gain fifteen thousand pounds by
the sale of thirty thousand copies.

When I began to write, I insured the house; and
suffered the utmost solicitude when I entrusted my

book to the carrier, though I had secured it against mischances by lodging two transcripts in different places. At my arrival, I expected that the patrons of learning would contend for the honour of a dedication, and resolved to maintain the dignity of letters, by a haughty contempt of pecuniary solicitations.

I took my lodgings near the house of the Royal Society, and expected every morning a visit from the president. I walked in the Park, and wondered that I overheard no mention of the great naturalist. At last I visited a noble earl, and told him of my work: he answered, that he was under an engagement never to subscribe. I was angry to have that refused which I did not mean to ask, and concealed my design of making him immortal. I went next day to another, and, in resentment of my late affront, offered to prefix his name to my new book. He said, coldly, that *he did not understand those things*; another thought, *there were too many books*; and another would *talk with me when the races were over*.

Being amazed to find a man of learning so indecently slighted, I resolved to indulge the philosophical pride of retirement and independence. I then sent to some of the principal booksellers the plan of my book, and bespoke a large room in the next tavern, that I might more commodiously see them together, and enjoy the contest, while they were outbidding one another. I drank my coffee, and yet nobody was come; at last I received a note from one, to tell me that he was going out of town; and from another, that natural history was out of his way. At last there came a grave man, who desired to see the work, and, without opening it, told me, that a book of that size *would never do*.

I then condescended to step into shops, and mentioned my work to the masters. Some never dealt with authors; others had their hands full; some never had known such a dead time; others had lost by all that they had published for the last twelvemonth. One offered to print my work, if I could procure subscriptions for five hundred, and would allow me two hundred copies for my property. I lost my patience, and gave him a kick; for which he has indicted me.

I can easily perceive, that there is a combination among them to defeat my expectations; and I find it so general, that I am sure it must have been long concerted. I suppose some of my friends, to whom I read the first part, gave notice of my design, and, perhaps, sold the treacherous intelligence at a higher price than the fraudulence of trade will now allow me for my book.

Inform me, Mr. Idler, what I must do; where must knowledge and industry find their recompense, thus neglected by the high, and cheated by the low? I sometimes resolve to print my book at my own expense, and, like the Sibyl, double the price; and sometimes am tempted, in emulation of Raleigh, to throw it into the fire, and leave this sordid generation to the curses of posterity. Tell me, dear Idler, what I shall do.

I am, Sir, &c.

No. 61. SATURDAY, JUNE 15, 1759.

MR. MINIM had now advanced himself to the zenith of critical reputation; when he was in the pit, every eye in the boxes was fixed upon him; when he entered his coffee-house, he was surrounded by circles of

candidates, who passed their noviciate of literature
under his tuition: his opinion was asked by all who
had no opinion of their own, and yet loved to debate
and decide; and no composition was supposed to pass
in safety to posterity, till it had been secured by
Minim's approbation.

Minim professes great admiration of the wisdom
and munificence by which the academies of the con-
tinent were raised; and often wishes for some standard
of taste, for some tribunal, to which merit may appeal
from caprice, prejudice and malignity. He has formed
a plan for an academy of criticism, where every work
of imagination may be read before it is printed, and
which shall authoritatively direct the theatres what
pieces to receive or reject, to exclude or to revive.

Such an institution would, in Dick's opinion, spread
the fame of English literature over Europe, and make
London the metropolis of elegance and politeness, the
place to which the learned and ingenious of all countries would repair for instruction and improvement,
and where nothing would any longer be applauded or
endured that was not conformed to the nicest rules,
and finished with the highest elegance.

Till some happy conjunction of the planets shall
dispose our princes or ministers to make themselves
immortal by such an academy, Minim contents himself to preside four nights in a week in a critical
society selected by himself, where he is heard without
contradiction, and whence his judgment is dissemi-
nated through the great vulgar and the small.

When he is placed in the chair of criticism, he
declares loudly for the noble simplicity of our an-
cestors, in opposition to the petty refinements, and

ornamental luxuriance. Sometimes he is sunk in despair, and perceives false delicacy daily gaining ground, and sometimes brightens his countenance with a gleam of hope, and predicts the revival of the true sublime. He then fulminates his loudest censures against the monkish barbarity of rhyme; wonders how beings that pretend to reason can be pleased with one line always ending like another; tells how unjustly and unnaturally sense is sacrificed to sound; how often the best thoughts are mangled by the necessity of confining or extending them to the dimensions of a couplet; and rejoices that genius has, in our days, shaken off the shackles which had encumbered it so long. Yet he allows that rhyme may sometimes be borne, if the lines be often broken, and the pauses judiciously diversified.

From blank verse he makes an easy transition to Milton, whom he produces as an example of the slow advance of lasting reputation. Milton is the only writer in whose books Minim can read for ever without weariness. What cause it is that exempts this pleasure from satiety he has long and diligently inquired, and believes it to consist in the perpetual variation of the numbers, by which the ear is gratified and the attention awakened. The lines that are commonly thought rugged and unmusical, he conceives to have been written to temper the melodious luxury of the rest, or to express things by a proper cadence: for he scarcely finds a verse that has not this favourite beauty; he declares that he could shiver in a hot-house when he reads that

the ground
Burns frore, and cold performs th' effect of fire;

and that, when Milton bewails his blindness, the verse,

So thick a drop serene has quench'd these orbs,

has, he knows not how, something that strikes him
with an obscure sensation like that which he fancies
would be felt from the sound of darkness.

Minim is not so confident of his rules of judgment
as not very eagerly to catch new light from the name
of the author. He is commonly so prudent as to spare
those whom he cannot resist, unless, as will sometimes
happen, he finds the publick combined against them.
But a fresh pretender to fame he is strongly inclined
to censure, till his own honour requires that he com-
mend him. Till he knows the success of a composition,
he intrenches himself in general terms; there are some
new thoughts and beautiful passages, but there is
likewise much which he would have advised the author
to expunge. He has several favourite epithets, of
which he has never settled the meaning, but which
are very commodiously applied to books which he
has not read, or cannot understand. One is *manly*,
another is *dry*, another *stiff*, and another *flimsy*; sometimes he discovers delicacy of style, and sometimes
meets with *strange expressions*.

He is never so great, or so happy, as when a youth
of promising parts is brought to receive his directions
for the prosecution of his studies. He then puts on
a very serious air; he advises the pupil to read none
but the best authors; and when he finds one congenial
to his own mind, to study his beauties, but avoid his
faults; and, when he sits down to write, to consider
how his favourite author would think at the present
time on the present occasion. He exhorts him to catch

those moments when he finds his thoughts expanded and his genius exalted, but to take care lest imagination hurry him beyond the bounds of nature. He holds diligence the mother of success; yet enjoins him, with great earnestness, not to read more than he can digest, and not to confuse his mind by pursuing studies of contrary tendencies. He tells him, that every man has his genius, and that Cicero could never be a poet. The boy retires illuminated, resolves to follow his genius, and to think how Milton would have thought: and Minim feasts upon his own beneficence till another day brings another pupil.

No. 71. SATURDAY, AUGUST 25, 1759.

Celan le selve angui, leoni, ed orsi
Dentro il lor verde.   TASSO, L'Aminta.

DICK SHIFTER was born in Cheapside, and, having passed reputably through all the classes of St. Paul's school, has been for some years a student in the Temple. He is of opinion, that intense application dulls the faculties, and thinks it necessary to temper the severity of the law by books that engage the mind, but do not fatigue it. He has, therefore, made a copious collection of plays, poems, and romances, to which he has recourse when he fancies himself tired with statutes and reports; and he seldom inquires very nicely whether he is weary or idle.

Dick has received from his favourite authors very strong impressions of a country life; and though his furthest excursions have been to Greenwich on one side, and Chelsea on the other, he has talked for several years, with great pomp of language and elevation of sentiments, about a state too high for contempt and too low for envy, about homely quiet and blameless simplicity, pastoral delights and rural innocence.

His friends, who had estates in the country, often invited him to pass the summer among them, but something or other had always hindered him; and he considered, that to reside in the house of another man was to incur a kind of dependence inconsistent with that laxity of life which he had imaged as the chief good.

This summer he resolved to be happy, and procured a lodging to be taken for him at a solitary house, situated about thirty miles from London, on the banks of a small river, with corn-fields before it and a hill on each side covered with wood. He concealed the place of his retirement, that none might violate his obscurity, and promised himself many a happy day when he should hide himself among the trees, and contemplate the tumults and vexations of the town.

He stepped into the post-chaise with his heart beating and his eyes sparkling, was conveyed through many varieties of delightful prospects, saw hills and meadows, cornfields and pasture, succeed each other, and for four hours charged none of his poets with fiction or exaggeration. He was now within six miles of happiness, when, having never felt so much agitation before, he began to wish his journey at an end, and the last hour was passed in changing his posture and quarrelling with his driver.

An hour may be tedious, but cannot be long. He at length alighted at his new dwelling, and was received as he expected; he looked round upon the hills and rivulets, but his joints were stiff and his muscles sore, and his first request was to see his bed-chamber.

He rested well, and ascribed the soundness of his sleep to the stillness of the country. He expected from that time nothing but nights of quiet and days of rapture, and, as soon as he had risen, wrote an account of his new state to one of his friends in the Temple.

"Dear Frank,

"I never pitied thee before. I am now, as I could wish every man of wisdom and virtue to be, in the regions of calm content and placid meditation; with all the beauties of nature soliciting my notice, and all the diversities of pleasure courting my acceptance; the birds are chirping in the hedges, and the flowers blooming in the mead; the breeze is whistling in the wood, and the sun dancing on the water. I can now say, with truth, that a man, capable of enjoying the purity of happiness, is never more busy than in his hours of leisure, nor ever less solitary than in a place of solitude.

I am, dear Frank, &c."

When he had sent away his letter, he walked into the wood, with some inconvenience, from the furze that pricked his legs, and the briars that scratched his face. He at last sat down under a tree, and heard with great delight a shower, by which he was not wet, rattling among the branches: This, said he, is the true image of obscurity; we hear of troubles and commotions, but never feel them.

His amusement did not overpower the calls of nature, and he, therefore, went back to order his dinner. He knew that the country produces whatever is eaten or drunk, and, imagining that he was now at the source of luxury, resolved to indulge himself with dainties which he supposed might be procured at a price next to nothing, if any price at all was expected; and intended to amaze the rusticks with his generosity, by paying more than they would ask. Of twenty dishes which he named, he was amazed to find that scarcely one was to be had; and heard, with astonishment and indignation, that all the fruits of the earth were sold at a higher price than in the streets of London.

His meal was short and sullen; and he retired again to his tree, to inquire how dearness could be consistent with abundance, or how fraud should be practised by simplicity. He was not satisfied with his own speculations, and, returning home early in the evening, went a while from window to window, and found that he wanted something to do.

He inquired for a newspaper, and was told that farmers never minded news, but that they could send for it from the alehouse. A messenger was despatched, who ran away at full speed, but loitered an hour behind the hedges, and at last coming back with his feet purposely bemired, instead of expressing the gratitude which Mr. Shifter expected for the bounty of a shilling, said, that the night was wet, and the way dirty, and he hoped that his worship would not think it much to give him half-a-crown.

Dick now went to bed with some abatement of his expectations; but sleep, I know not how, revives our hopes, and rekindles our desires. He rose early in the morning, surveyed the landscape, and was pleased. He walked out, and passed from field to field, without observing any beaten path, and wondered that he had not seen the shepherdesses dancing, nor heard the swains piping to their flocks.

At last he saw some reapers and harvest-women at dinner. Here, said he, are the true Arcadians; and advanced courteously towards them, as afraid of confusing them by the dignity of his presence. They acknowledged his superiority by no other token than that of asking him for something to drink. He imagined that he had now purchased the privilege of discourse, and began to descend to familiar questions, endeavouring to accommodate his discourse to the grossness of rustick understandings. The clowns soon found, that he did not know wheat from rye, and began to despise him; one of the boys, by pretending to show him a bird's nest, decoyed him into a ditch; and one of the wenches sold him a bargain.

This walk had given him no great pleasure; but he hoped to find other rusticks less coarse of manners, and less mischievous of disposition. Next morning he was accosted by an attorney, who told him that, unless he made farmer Dobson satisfaction for trampling his grass, he had orders to indict him. Shifter was offended, but not terrified; and, telling the attorney that he was himself a lawyer, talked so volubly of pettyfoggers and barrators, that he drove him away.

Finding his walks thus interrupted, he was inclined to ride, and, being pleased with the appearance of a horse that was grazing in a neighbouring meadow, inquired the owner, who warranted him sound, and would not sell him, but that he was too fine for a plain man. Dick paid down the price, and, riding out to enjoy the evening, fell with his new horse into a ditch; they got out with difficulty, and, as he was going to mount again, a countryman looked at the horse, and perceived him to be blind. Dick went to the seller, and demanded back his money; but was told, that a man who rented his ground must do the best for himself; that his landlord had his rent though the year was barren; and that, whether horses had eyes or no, he should sell them to the highest bidder.

Shifter now began to be tired with rustick simplicity, and on the fifth day took possession again of his chambers, and bade farewell to the regions of calm content and placid meditation.

No. 85. SATURDAY, DECEMBER 1, 1759.

ONE of the peculiarities which distinguish the present age is the multiplication of books. Every day brings new advertisements of literary undertakings, and we are flattered with repeated promises of growing wise on easier terms than our progenitors.

How much either happiness or knowledge is advanced by this multitude of authors, it is not very easy to decide.

He that teaches us any thing which we knew not before, is undoubtedly to be reverenced as a master.

He that conveys knowledge by more pleasing ways, may very properly be loved as a benefactor; and he that supplies life with innocent amusement, will be certainly caressed as a pleasing companion.

But few of those who fill the world with books have any pretensions to the hope either of pleasing or instructing. They have often no other task than to lay two books before them, out of which they compile a third, without any new materials of their own, and with very little application of judgment to those which former authors have supplied.

That all compilations are useless, I do not assert. Particles of science are often very widely scattered. Writers of extensive comprehension have incidental remarks upon topicks very remote from the principal subject, which are often more valuable than formal treatises, and which yet are not known because they are not promised in the title. He that collects those under proper heads is very laudably employed, for, though he exerts no great abilities in the work, he facilitates the progress of others, and by making that easy of attainment which is already written, may give some mind, more vigorous or more adventurous than his own, leisure for new thoughts and original designs.

But the collections poured lately from the press have been seldom made at any great expense of time or inquiry, and, therefore, only serve to distract choice without supplying any real want.

It is observed that "a corrupt society has many laws"; I know not whether it is not equally true, that "an ignorant age has many books." When the treasures of ancient knowledge lie unexamined, and original authors are neglected and forgotten, compilers and plagiaries are encouraged, who give us again what we had before, and grow great by setting before us what our own sloth had hidden from our view.

Yet are not even these writers to be indiscriminately censured and rejected. Truth like beauty varies its fashions, and is best recommended by different dresses to different minds; and he that recalls the attention of mankind to any part of learning which time has left behind it, may be truly said to advance the literature of his own age. As the manners of nations vary, new topicks of persuasion become necessary, and new combinations of imagery are produced; and he that can accommodate himself to the reigning taste, may always have readers who, perhaps, would not have looked upon better performances.

To exact of every man who writes, that he should say something new, would be to reduce authors to a small number; to oblige the most fertile genius to say only what is new would be to contract his volumes to a few pages. Yet, surely, there ought to be some bounds to repetition; libraries ought no more to be heaped for ever with the same thoughts differently expressed, than with the same books differently decorated.

The good or evil which these secondary writers produce is seldom of any long duration. As they owe their existence to change of fashion, they commonly disappear when a new fashion becomes prevalent. The authors that in any nation last from age to age are very few, because there are very few that have any other claim to notice than that they catch hold on present curiosity, and gratify some accidental desire, or produce some temporary conveniency.

But however the writers of the day may despair of future fame, they ought at least to forbear any present mischief. Though they cannot arrive at eminent heights of excellence, they might keep themselves harmless. They might take care to inform themselves before they attempt to inform others, and exert the little influence which they have for honest purposes.

But such is the present state of our literature, that the ancient sage, who thought *a great book a great evil*, would now think the multitude of books a multitude of evils. He would consider a bulky writer who engrossed a year, and a swarm of pamphleteers who stole each an hour, as equal wasters of human life, and would make no other difference between them, than between a beast of prey and a flight of locusts.

No. 97. SATURDAY, FEBRUARY 23, 1760.

IT may, I think, be justly observed, that few books disappoint their readers more than the narrations of travellers. One part of mankind is naturally curious to learn the sentiments, manners, and condition of the rest; and every mind that has leisure or power to extend its views, must be desirous of knowing in what proportion Providence has distributed the blessings of nature, or the advantages of art, among the several nations of the earth.

This general desire easily procures readers to every book from which it can expect gratification. The adventurer upon unknown coasts, and the describer of distant regions, is always welcomed as a man who has laboured for the pleasure of others, and who is able to enlarge our knowledge and rectify our opinions; but when the volume is opened, nothing is found but such general accounts as leave no distinct idea behind them, or such minute enumerations as few can read with either profit or delight.

Every writer of travels should consider, that, like all other authors, he undertakes either to instruct or please, or to mingle pleasure with instruction. He that instructs must offer to the mind something to be imitated, or something to be avoided; he that pleases must offer new images to his reader, and enable him to form a tacit comparison of his own state with that of others.

The greater part of travellers tell nothing, because their method of travelling supplies them with nothing to be told. He that enters a town at night, and surveys it in the morning, and then hastens away to another place, and guesses at the manners of the inhabitants by the entertainment which his inn afforded him, may please himself for a time with a hasty change of scenes, and a confused remembrance of palaces and churches; he may gratify his eye with a variety of landscapes, and regale his palate with a succession of vintages; but let him be contented to please himself without endeavouring to disturb others. Why should he record excursions by which nothing could be learned, or wish to make a show of knowledge, which, without some power of intuition unknown to other mortals, he never could attain?

Of those who crowd the world with their itineraries, some have no other purpose than to describe the face of the country; those who sit idle at home, and are curious to know what is done or suffered in distant countries, may be informed by one of these wanderers, that on a certain day he set out early with the caravan, and in the first hour's march saw, towards the south, a hill covered with trees, then passed over a stream, which ran northward with a swift course, but which is probably dry in the summer months; that an hour after he saw something to the right which looked at a distance like a castle with towers, but which he discovered afterwards to be a craggy rock; that he then entered a valley, in which he saw several trees tall and flourishing, watered by a rivulet not marked in the maps, of which he was not able to learn the name; that the road afterward grew stony, and the country uneven, where he observed among the hills many hollows worn by torrents, and was told that the road was passable only part of the year; that going on they found the remains of a building, once, perhaps, a fortress to secure the pass, or to restrain the robbers, of which the present inhabitants can give no other account than that it is haunted by fairies; that they went to dine at the foot of a rock, and travelled the rest of the day along the banks of a river, from which the road turned aside towards evening, and brought them within sight of a village, which was once a considerable town, but which afforded them neither good victuals nor commodious lodging.

Thus he conducts his reader through wet and dry, over rough and smooth, without incidents, without reflection; and, if he obtains his company for another day, will dismiss him again at night, equally fatigued with a like succession of rocks and streams, mountains and ruins.

This is the common style of those sons of enterprise, who visit savage countries, and range through solitude and desolation; who pass a desert, and tell that it is sandy; who cross a valley, and find that it is green. There are others of more delicate sensibility, that visit only the realms of elegance and softness; that wander through Italian palaces, and amuse the gentle reader with catalogues of pictures; that hear masses in magnificent churches, and recount the number of the pillars or variegations of the pavement. And there are yet others, who, in disdain of trifles, copy inscriptions elegant and rude, ancient and modern; and transcribe into their book the walls of every edifice, sacred or civil. He that reads these books must consider his labour as its own reward; for he will find nothing on which attention can fix, or which memory can retain.

He that would travel for the entertainment of others, should remember that the great object of remark is human life. Every nation has something peculiar in its manufactures, its works of genius, its medicines, its agriculture, its customs and its policy. He only is a useful traveller, who brings home something by which his country may be benefited; who procures some supply of want, or some mitigation of evil, which may enable his readers to compare their condition with that of others, to improve it whenever it is worse, and whenever it is better to enjoy it.

No. 103. SATURDAY, APRIL 5, 1760.

Respicere ad longæ jussit spatia ultima vitæ.
Juv. Sat. x. 275.

MUCH of the pain and pleasure of mankind arises from the conjectures which every one makes of the thoughts of others; we all enjoy praise which we do not hear, and resent contempt which we do not see. The Idler may, therefore, be forgiven, if he suffers his imagination to represent to him what his readers will say or think when they are informed that they have now his last paper in their hands.

Value is more frequently raised by scarcity than by

use. That which lay neglected when it was common, rises in estimation as its quantity becomes less. We seldom learn the true want of what we have till it is discovered that we can have no more.

This essay will, perhaps, be read with care even by those who have not yet attended to any other; and he that finds this late attention recompensed, will not forbear to wish that he had bestowed it sooner.

Though the Idler and his readers have contracted no close friendship, they are, perhaps, both unwilling to part. There are few things not purely evil, of which we can say, without some emotion of uneasiness, *this is the last*. Those who never could agree together, shed tears when mutual discontent has determined them to final separation; of a place which has been frequently visited, though without pleasure, the last look is taken with heaviness of heart; and the Idler, with all his chilness of tranquillity, is not wholly un-affected by the thought that his last essay is now before him.

The secret horrour of the last is inseparable from a thinking being, whose life is limited, and to whom death is dreadful. We always make a secret comparison between a part and the whole; the termination of any period of life reminds us that life itself has likewise its termination; when we have done any thing for the last time, we involuntarily reflect that a part of the days allotted us is past, and that as more is past there is less remaining.

It is very happily and kindly provided, that in every life there are certain pauses and interruptions, which force consideration upon the careless, and seriousness upon the light; points of time where one course of

action ends, and another begins; and by vicissitudes
of fortune or alteration of employment, by change of
place or loss of friendship, we are forced to say of
something, *this is the last.*

An even and unvaried tenour of life always hides
from our apprehension the approach of its end. Succession is not perceived but by variation; he that lives
to-day as he lived yesterday, and expects that, as the
present day is, such will be the morrow, easily conceives time as running in a circle and returning to
itself. The uncertainty of our duration is impressed
commonly by dissimilitude of condition; it is only by
finding life changeable that we are reminded of its
shortness.

This conviction, however forcible at every new im-
pression, is every moment fading from the mind; and
partly by the inevitable incursion of new images, and
partly by voluntary exclusion of unwelcome thoughts,
we are again exposed to the universal fallacy; and we
must do another thing for the last time, before we
consider that the time is nigh when we shall do no
more.

As the last Idler is published in that solemn week
which the Christian world has always set apart for
the examination of the conscience, the review of life,
the extinction of earthly desires, and the renovation
of holy purposes; I hope that my readers are already
disposed to view every incident with seriousness, and
improve it by meditation; and that, when they see
this series of trifles brought to a conclusion, they will
consider that, by outliving the Idler, they have passed
weeks, months and years, which are now no longer in
their power; that an end must in time be put to every

thing great as to every thing little; that to life must come its last hour, and to this system of being its last day, the hour at which probation ceases, and repentance will be vain; the day in which every work of the hand, and imagination of the heart shall be brought to judgment, and an everlasting futurity shall be determined by the past.

CAMBRIDGE
PLAIN TEXTS

~~

The following Volumes are the latest
additions to this Series:

English

French

German

Spanish

small octavo pages of text, preceded
note on the author

LIMP CLOTH

German

GRILLPARZER. Der Arme Spielmann *and* Erinnerungen an
Beethoven.
HERDER. Kleinere Aufsätze I.
HOFFMANN. Der Kampf der Sänger.
LESSING. Hamburgische Dramaturgie I.
LESSING. Hamburgische Dramaturgie II.

Italian

ALFIERI. La Virtù Sconosciuta.
GOZZI, GASPARO. La Gazzetta Veneta.
LEOPARDI. Pensieri.
MAZZINI. Fede e Avvenire.
ROSMINI. Cinque Piaghe.

Spanish

BOLÍVAR, SIMÓN. Address to the Venezuelan Congress
at Angostura, February 15, 1819.
CALDERÓN. La Cena de Baltasar.
CERVANTES. Prologues and Epilogue.
CERVANTES. Rinconete y Cortadillo.
ESPRONCEDA. El Estudiante de Salamanca.
LOPE DE VEGA. El Mejor Alcalde, el Rey.
LUIS DE LEÓN. Poesías Originales.
OLD SPANISH BALLADS.
VILLEGAS. El Abencerraje.
VILLENA: LEBRIJA: ENCINA. Selections.

SOME PRESS OPINIONS

"These are delightful, slim little books....The print is very clear and pleasant to the eye....These Cambridge Plain Texts are just the kind of book that a lover of letters longs to put in his pocket as a prophylactic against boredom." THE NEW STATESMAN

"These little books...are exquisitely printed on excellent paper and are prefaced in each case by a brief biographical note concerning the author: otherwise entirely unencumbered with notes or explanatory matter, they form the most delicious and companionable little volumes we remember to have seen. The title-page is a model of refined taste—*simplex munditiis*." THE ANGLO-FRENCH REVIEW

"With their admirable print, the little books do credit to the great Press which is responsible for them."
NOTES AND QUERIES

"The series of texts of notable Italian works which is being issued at Cambridge should be made known wherever there is a chance of studying the language; they are clear, in a handy form, and carefully edited....The venture deserves well of all who aim at the higher culture."
THE INQUIRER

"Selections of this kind, made by competent hands, may serve to make us acquainted with much that we should otherwise miss. To read two of Donne's tremendous sermons may send many readers eagerly to enlarge their knowledge of one of the great glories of the English pulpit." THE HOLBORN REVIEW

"This new Spanish text-book, printed on excellent paper, in delightfully clear type and of convenient pocket size, preserves the high level of achievement that characterises the series." THE TEACHER'S WORLD *on* "Cervantes: Prologues and Epilogue"

"It is difficult to praise too highly the Cambridge Plain Texts." THE LONDON MERCURY

www.ingramcontent.com/pod-product-compliance
Ingram Content Group UK Ltd.
Pitfield, Milton Keynes, MK11 3LW, UK
UKHW042148280225
455719UK00001B/190